9.0

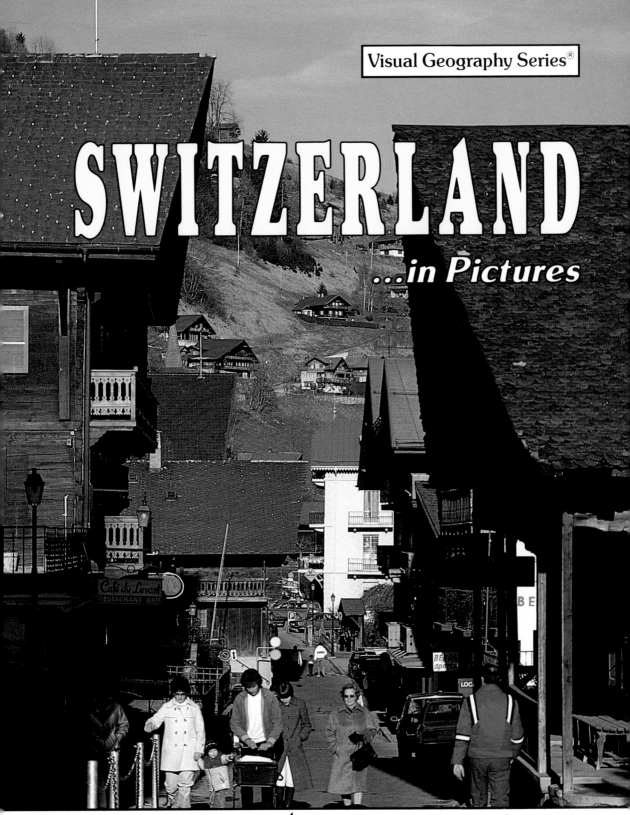

Visual Geography Series®

SWITZERLAND
...in Pictures

Prepared by
Geography Department

Lerner Publications Company
Minneapolis

VISUAL GEOGRAPHY SERIES®

Publisher
Harry Jonas Lerner
Senior Editor
Mary M. Rodgers
Editor
Lori Ann Coleman
Photo Researcher
Beth Johnson
Consultants/Contributors
Frank Jossi
Sandra K. Davis
Designer
Jim Simondet
Cartographer
Carol F. Barrett
Indexer
Sylvia Timian
Production Manager
Gary J. Hansen

Independent Picture Service

People in wild costumes celebrate the arrival of spring in central Switzerland with a lively outdoor dance.

This book is an all-new edition of the Visual Geography Series. Previous editions were published by Sterling Publishing Company, New York City. The text, set in 10/12 Century Textbook, is fully revised and updated, and new photographs, maps, charts, and captions have been added.

LIBRARY OF CONGRESS CATALOGING-IN-PUBLICATION DATA

Switzerland in pictures / prepared by Geography Department, Lerner Publications Company.
   p. cm.—(Visual Geography Series)
   Includes index.
   ISBN 0–8225–1895–3 (lib. bdg.)
   1. Switzerland—Geography. 2. Switzerland—Pictorial works. [Switzerland.] I. Lerner Publications Company. Geography Dept. II. Series: Visual geography series (Minneapolis, Minn.)
DQ20.S85   1996
949.4—dc20
                    95–2807
                    CIP
                    AC

International Standard Book Number: 0–8225–1895–3
Library of Congress Catalog Card Number: 95–2807

Independent Picture Service

A group of elderly Swiss gathers for a chess game in a park in Zurich, a city in northern Switzerland.

Acknowledgments

Title page photo by Mark Kimak.

Elevation contours adapted from *The Times Atlas of the World,* seventh comprehensive edition (New York: Times Books, 1985).

1 2 3 4 5 6 – JR – 01 00 99 98 97 96

Youngsters enjoy a toboggan ride in Davos, in eastern Switzerland.

Contents

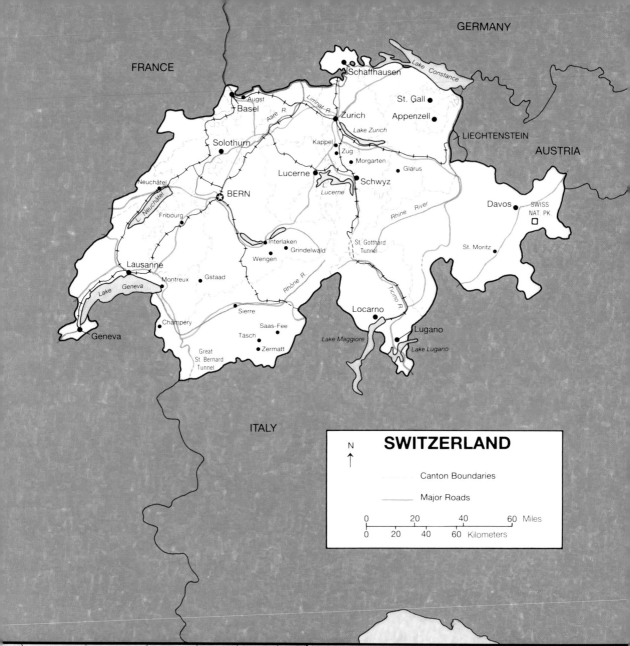

GERMANY

FRANCE

Schaffhausen

Lake Constance

Basel
Augst

Aare R.

Limmat R.

Zurich

St. Gall

Appenzell

Solothurn

Kappel

Lake Zurich

LIECHTENSTEIN

AUSTRIA

Neuchâtel

L. Neuchâtel

Fribourg

BERN

Lucerne

Zug

Morgarten

Schwyz

Glarus

L. Lucerne

Rhine River

Davos

SWISS
NAT. PK.

Lausanne

Interlaken

Grindelwald

St. Gotthard
Tunnel

St. Moritz

Montreux

Gstaad

Wengen

Rhône R.

Lake Geneva

Sierre

Champéry

Saas-Fee

Täsch

Zermatt

Geneva

Great
St. Bernard
Tunnel

Locarno

Lake Maggiore

Ticino R.

Lugano

Lake Lugano

ITALY

SWITZERLAND

N ↑

Canton Boundaries

Major Roads

0	20	40	60 Miles
0	20	40	60 Kilometers

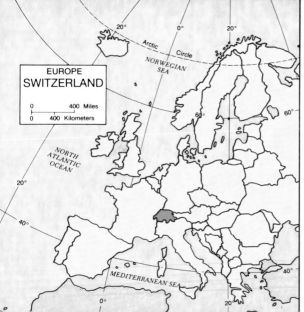

EUROPE
SWITZERLAND

0	400 Miles
0	400 Kilometers

ARCTIC Circle
NORWEGIAN SEA

NORTH
ATLANTIC
OCEAN

MEDITERRANEAN SEA

METRIC CONVERSION CHART
To Find Approximate Equivalents

WHEN YOU KNOW:	MULTIPLY BY:	TO FIND:
AREA		
acres	0.41	hectares
square miles	2.59	square kilometers
CAPACITY		
gallons	3.79	liters
LENGTH		
feet	30.48	centimeters
yards	0.91	meters
miles	1.61	kilometers
MASS (weight)		
pounds	0.45	kilograms
tons	0.91	metric tons
VOLUME		
cubic yards	0.77	cubic meters
TEMPERATURE		
degrees Fahrenheit	0.56 (*after* subtracting 32)	degrees Celsius

Women in traditional dress lead a parade through the streets of Sierre, a town in the Swiss Alps.

Introduction

Switzerland, a small and mountainous country in central Europe, shares a common history and ethnic identity with many of its neighbors. The Swiss fell under the domain of two separate early realms—the Roman Empire and the Holy Roman Empire—before forming a loose confederation of cantons (territorial divisions) in the thirteenth century. As a semi-independent part of the Holy Roman Empire, the confederation suffered political and religious strife. For centuries the Habsburgs—a powerful family of rulers that reigned over the Holy Roman Empire and Austria—tried unsuccessfully to gain full control of the Swiss Confederation.

The strife continued in the 1500s, when Switzerland and much of Europe experienced religious change during the Protestant Reformation. This religious movement aimed at resolving serious problems within the Roman Catholic Church. The movement came to a head in Switzerland with the development of a new form of Christianity called Protestantism. The Reformation eventually divided Protestants from Catholics and caused armed conflicts between the two groups on several occasions.

After coming to terms with religious differences, the Swiss faced another threat from outside their borders. In the late

5

1700s, Switzerland came under the control of the French leader Napoleon Bonaparte. The French imposed a central government on the Swiss cantons and wrote a Swiss constitution. When European powers eventually defeated Napoleon, they officially recognized Switzerland's independence. These powers also accepted Switzerland's strict policy of neutrality, under which the country would not take sides in any international conflict.

Switzerland's neutrality did not keep the country from involvement in European affairs, however. During World War I (1914–1918) and World War II (1939–1945), for example, the Swiss took in refugees and provided medical aid to anyone who needed it.

In addition to struggling for political independence, the Swiss have also been challenged by the diversity of their nation's population. Switzerland has three official languages—German, French, and Italian, which mirror its ethnic makeup. To balance the interests of the different ethnic groups, the Swiss constitution gives each canton a great deal of local decision-making authority. By remaining neutral and by allowing the cantons to share political power with the national government, Switzerland has enjoyed relative peace for many years.

Political stability has also allowed this once-poor country to develop a strong industrial base. As a result, Switzerland is among the leading makers of engineering equipment and watches and has one of the world's best-developed banking systems. A strong economy has rewarded the Swiss with one of the highest standards of living in the world.

Even so, Switzerland has challenges to face in the future. Debates among Swiss citizens revolve around issues of immigration policy, unity with the rest of Europe, rising crime, and growing health problems. Yet Switzerland is perhaps the world's best example of how a multilingual and ethnically diverse nation can live and prosper in harmony.

Students wait for a train after a weeklong hiking trip in the mountains.

A chapel overlooks a calm lake in the Swiss Alps. Besides Switzerland, the Alps mountain system mainly covers parts of France, Italy, Austria, Slovenia, Albania, and Montenegro.

1) The Land

A small, landlocked nation in central Europe, Switzerland covers 15,939 square miles—an area about twice the size of the state of West Virginia. Switzerland's neighbors include Italy to the south and Austria to the east. Germany lies across Switzerland's northern boundary, with France to the west. Liechtenstein, a small independent principality (a realm ruled by a prince), carves out a spot on the Swiss-Austrian border.

Topography

Switzerland's uneven terrain is dominated by the Alps, Europe's largest mountain system. The Swiss portion of the Alps stretches across the southern part of the nation. Another chain, the Jura Mountains, extends across northwestern Switzerland. The Mittelland (middle land), a central plateau that is home to the majority of Swiss citizens, is a series of hills and plains sandwiched between the two mountain ranges. Although the Swiss Alps cover more than 60 percent of the country, only 20 percent of the population live among the towering peaks.

The Alps form a vast mountain range 500 miles long and 160 miles wide in south central Europe. The rugged chain stretches eastward from France into Switzerland,

7

The Matterhorn juts through the clouds in the Pennine Alps. Climbers first scaled this majestic peak in 1865. Nowadays about 2,000 people reach the mountain's summit each year.

northern Italy, western Austria, and northern Slovenia. Within Switzerland the Alps run from the southwest to the northeast through the southern two-thirds of the country and contain some of the highest peaks in Europe. More than 50 mountains in the Swiss Alps reach or exceed 12,000 feet in elevation.

The Swiss Alps are actually two parallel sets of mountain ranges divided by wide river valleys. The northern Swiss Alps include the Bernese Alps in the west and the Glarus Alps to the east. The northern ranges have only two natural passes and contain two major peaks, Finsteraarhorn and Jungfrau, which are both part of the Bernese range. Major resort centers nestled among the northern Swiss Alps attract visitors from around the world. Interlaken, Gstaad, Wengen, and Grindelwald offer some of the world's best skiing.

The Pennine, Lepontine, and Rhaetian ranges make up the southern Swiss Alps. The Pennine Alps, which straddle the Swiss-Italian frontier, boast the Matterhorn, a famous summit that rises 14,692 feet along the border. Nearby, the Dufourspitze (15,203 feet), Switzerland's highest point, soars from the top of Monte Rosa, a mountain with several high peaks.

The Simplon, Furka, and St. Gotthard passes provide routes through the southern Alps. Some passes are often closed in winter because of avalanches and other dangerous snow conditions. But trains designed to climb the mountains carry vacationers to Zermatt, a resort near the Matterhorn, year-round. Besides the numerous resorts, many villages and small towns lie in valleys throughout the Swiss Alps, where farmers mainly raise livestock to make a living.

The Jura Mountains, in the northwest, have lower elevations than the Alps do. The peaks of the Juras average about 3,000 to 4,000 feet above sea level. The region has thick pine forests, lush pastures, and only a few large communities. Forests in the Jura region supply the small Swiss timber industry with lumber, but horse breeding and watchmaking are the main economic activities. Vineyards thrive in the foothills south of Neuchâtel, a sizable city on the northern shore of Lake Neuchâtel.

The Mittelland—with its rolling hills, fertile plains, and large lakes—holds most of the Swiss population. The central plateau boasts several of Switzerland's major cities, such as Bern (the Swiss capital), Lucerne, and Zurich. The region receives water from the Aare River, a tributary of the Rhine. Plenty of water, along with fertile soil, has made the Mittelland Switzerland's most productive agricultural area, specializing in mainly grain and fruit crops.

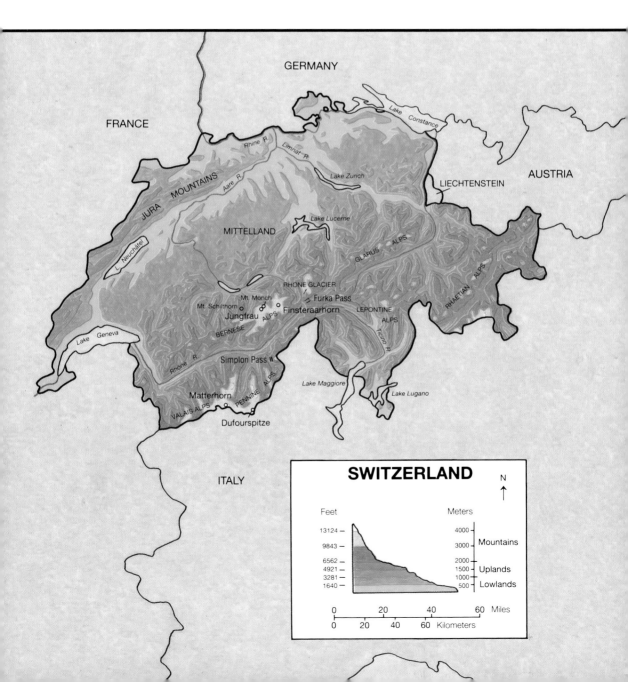

Rivers and Lakes

Switzerland benefits from an extensive system of waterways, most of which flow out of its mountain ranges. Rising in the Swiss Alps, the Rhine River travels eastward, carving a valley between the Glarus Alps to the north and the Lepontine and Rhaetian alps to the south. The Rhine's 820-mile course then takes it north along the Swiss border with Liechtenstein. The waterway then flows into Lake Constance, exits to the west, and runs along the western edge of Germany to the North Sea.

The other major rivers in Switzerland are the Rhône, the Aare, and the Ticino.

The Rhône River begins as a trickle at the Rhône Glacier (ice mass) in southwestern Switzerland. The waterway then broadens in a valley between the Bernese and the Pennine Alps before flowing through Lake Geneva and west through southern France into the Mediterranean Sea. The Aare River forms in the Alps, travels north, and passes through Bern before joining with the Rhine River on the northern Swiss border. The Ticino River flows through the mountains of southern Switzerland into Lake Maggiore on the Italian border.

The Alpine rivers, which travel in many different directions, together serve as one of Europe's major watersheds. Dams built

Photo by Bernice Condit

A monument on the Rhine River in northern Switzerland marks the spot where Switzerland, France, and Germany meet. The Rhine is an important transportation link for all three countries.

The melting waters of the Rhône Glacier, a huge ice mass in the Swiss Alps, form the beginning of the Rhône River.

along many Alpine streams generate hydroelectric power for Swiss industries.

Thousands of years ago, melting glaciers formed several large lakes in the Mittelland. From southwest to northeast, these lakes include Lake Geneva, Lake Lucerne, Lake Zurich, and Lake Constance. Separating the Mitteland from the Jura in northwestern Switzerland is Lake Neuchâtel.

Climate

The mountains of Switzerland influence the climate of the country. For example, temperatures fall with a rise in altitude. As a result, the Mittelland and the valleys between the peaks of the Juras and the Alps are typically warmer than mountainous areas are. Fog often hovers over low-lying areas in Switzerland, while at higher altitudes, the weather is usually sunny.

Precipitation—mainly rain and snow— is ample in Switzerland, averaging 39 inches per year. Levels vary by region, however, with the largest amounts falling in the mountains. Valleys surrounded by the highest summits generally receive the least amount of precipitation. Snow covers the highest Swiss peaks for more than half the year.

A warm wind known as the foehn sometimes blows through the Swiss Alps from the south, causing sudden temperature changes. Foehn winds usually occur in spring, bringing warm weather that rapidly melts Alpine snow and can cause avalanches.

Summer generally features mild temperatures in the Mittelland. In Bern the average July temperature is 70° F. Geneva, a large city in the south, stays a few degrees warmer than most of the rest of the country and is mild enough to support palm trees, which line Lake Geneva. Summer temperatures at St. Moritz in the Rhaetian Alps are cool, averaging about 63° F in July.

Switzerland's winters bring great piles of snow. Winter is cold, wet, and foggy in the Mittelland. In the Alps, deep snow blankets the mountains and glaciers beneath a normally clear sky. Winter temperatures average about 35° F in Bern. At St. Moritz, January temperatures hover around 29° F. To the south of the tallest Alpine peaks, temperatures regularly exceed 40° F, even during the coldest winter months.

11

Forests cover much of the Jura region. Like many of Switzerland's woodlands, these forests have been damaged by acid rain—a mixture of rain and airborne pollution.

Lush vegetation thrives in the warm, moist climate of southern Switzerland.

Flora and Fauna

Because of the country's varying levels of elevation, Switzerland has several belts of vegetation. In the north, at the lowest elevations—less than 1,800 feet above sea level—chestnut, cypress, almond, and walnut trees can be found. In the south at this elevation, palm, fig, and orange trees thrive. From 1,800 feet to 4,000 feet, beech, oak and maple trees abound. Pine and fir trees, rhododendrons, and larches flourish at higher altitudes.

At 10,000 feet, trees give way to Alpine pastures and grassy meadows featuring eidelweiss, alpenroses, primroses, mountain poppies, and other hardy wildflowers. Switzerland's forests cover only about one-fourth of the country, and many of the trees have been damaged by acid rain, a toxic result of air pollution that has severely affected the Swiss countryside.

Centuries of hunting and development have depleted Switzerland's wildlife. Most wild animals live in the Alps. Rabbits, foxes, badgers, marmots, deer, chamois (an antelopelike creature), otters, and several kinds of birds populate the country. The round ibex, reintroduced after dying out in Switzerland, can also be found in the Alps. Swiss laws protect most animals and allow for only a short hunting season. In far eastern Switzerland lies the Swiss National Park, a 70-square-mile area where strict rules preserve the wildlife.

Cities

More than two-thirds of Switzerland's seven million people live in cities, most of which are concentrated around Lake Geneva and throughout the Mittelland. Even with this concentration in the central region, only metropolitan Zurich has more than one million residents. Bern and Geneva, though smaller in size, still are key international centers of commerce, culture, and industry.

Switzerland's diverse urban areas are dominated by different ethnic groups and languages. For example, German is spoken in Zurich, Bern, and Basel, while

Courtesy of Swiss National Tourist Office

An Alpine marmot stands guard atop a rock. Marmots are members of the squirrel species.

French is the most commonly heard language in Geneva. Residents of Lugano, in southern Switzerland, speak Italian.

ZURICH

Zurich, a city of 835,000 people at the northern tip of Lake Zurich, is Switzerland's largest urban area. Settlers came to

Photo © Ulrich Tutsch

Transportation routes line the shores of Lake Geneva in southwestern Switzerland. Ferry services, railroads, and highways link the region's many towns with its two main cities—Geneva and Lausanne.

Illuminated at night, the Grossmünster Cathedral in Zurich lights up the Limnat River.

Zurich as early as 4500 B.C. to plant wheat and to raise cattle and pigs. A province of the Roman Empire by the first century A.D., the area was known as Turicum. By the twelfth century, Zurich had developed into a major trading hub for the exchange of silk, linen, wool, and leather.

In the 1300s, Zurich joined the Swiss Confederation, the union of cantons that eventually became Switzerland. Zurich developed into a center of German culture and literature, as well as into a key industrial city. Textiles, engineering, and finance have become Zurich's core industries. In fact, the city's stock exchange ranks fourth in the world, after those in New York, London, and Tokyo.

With expensive stores and excellent museums, Zurich is one of Europe's most famous hubs. The city's main boulevard, the Bahnhofstrasse, stretches from the historic railway station through the downtown area to Lake Zurich. The arts community revolves around the Swiss Na-

Boat owners in Zurich dock their watercrafts along the Limnat River.

tional Museum and the Kunsthaus, a modern art museum with works by many internationally renowned artists.

The Grossmünster Cathedral and the Fraumünster Church stand on opposite sides of the Limnat River, which flows north from Lake Zurich. Zurich is also home to the Federal Institute of Technology, a world-famous scientific school, and to the University of Zurich, Switzerland's largest institution of higher learning.

Although Zurich has a strong cultural and economic base, the city has recently faced mounting problems related to drug trafficking and AIDS (acquired immune deficiency syndrome), a disease linked to the use of dirty needles by drug addicts. To control crime and drug abuse, officials have cracked down on the Platzspitz—a park in central Zurich where users were officially free to buy, sell, and inject drugs.

SECONDARY CITIES

The capital of Switzerland, Bern (metropolitan population 300,000) lies on a peninsula overlooking the Aare River in the center of the Mittelland. Bern was a political hub of German Alemanni tribes in the twelfth century. Much of its downtown area dates to the fifteenth century, after a major fire forced the city to rebuild. Bern became the capital of the Swiss Confederation in 1848.

Fancy buildings, ornate fountains, and many historical structures adorn the streets of Bern. The Zeitglockenturm, a clock tower built in 1530, features moving wooden figures that appear when the clock strikes. Several pits that house bears—the city's symbol—are dug into a popular square in Bern, whose name is derived from the German word for bears. The Swiss national parliament building, the

Photo by Archive Photos/Bill Bardsley

The Bundeshaus, or federal parliament building, was built in Bern in the late 1800s. Residents of Bern—Switzerland's capital—celebrated the city's 800th birthday in 1991.

Docked at Geneva, a cruise ship *(left)* offers sightseers a view of the Jet d'Eau, a fountain that spurts water nearly 500 feet into the air. Small hotels line part of Geneva's lakefront *(below)*.

Courtesy of Swiss National Tourist Office

Bundeshaus, is also located in Bern and is the workplace of the country's legislature.

Lying in southwestern Switzerland near the French border, Geneva (metropolitan population 379,000) is the home of many international organizations, including the International Red Cross, the International Labor Organization, the World Health Organization, and the World Council of Churches. The Palais des Nations is the European headquarters of the United Nations.

Many employees of Geneva's international organizations and other firms come as guest workers from outside Switzerland. Besides hosting international agencies, Geneva produces expensive watches, clocks, and jewelry. A thriving tourism industry also benefits the city's economy.

Divided by the Rhône River, Geneva has an old section and a new section. The older part of the city features historical buildings, such as St. Peter's Cathedral, begun in the A.D. 900s. The University of Geneva and the town hall, both built in the 1500s, also stand in this section of the

Photo by Mary Ney

city. North of the Rhône lies the newer part of town, where more modern architecture houses a number of international firms and agencies.

The city of Basel (metropolitan population 362,000) straddles the Rhine River in northwestern Switzerland. An age-old religious center, Basel joined the Swiss Confederation in 1501. The city is an important banking and industrial hub that also manufactures chemicals and pharmaceuticals. The University of Basel, built in 1460, is the oldest institution of higher learning in Switzerland. The university has an international reputation for research.

Lugano (metropolitan population 94,000), the largest city in the Italian-speaking canton of Ticino, lies on the shores of Lake Lugano in the extreme south of Switzerland. The city has been inhabited for more than 2,300 years. After centuries under Roman and Italian rule, Lugano was absorbed by the Swiss Confederation in the 1500s. The city later became part of the canton of Ticino in 1803, when Ticino officially joined Switzerland. The chief economic activities in Lugano are tourism, banking, and manufacturing—especially of chocolate and tobacco products.

Courtesy of Swiss National Tourist Office

Outdoor diners enjoy the warm, sunny weather in Lugano.

Photo © Luke Golobitsh

Carrying on a tradition that began centuries ago, the city of Basel hired Swiss sculptor Jean Tinguely to create this fountain in the 1960s. Elaborate fountains adorn many of Basel's city squares.

17

Ancient settlements in Switzerland were concentrated around the region's many lakes. The fertile countryside and fish-filled waters provided the inhabitants of these villages with plenty of food.

2) History and Government

Because of its location in central Europe, Switzerland sits at a continental cross-roads. As a result, many peoples have visited, settled, or conquered the country. The first evidence of human beings in Switzerland comes from artifacts of an unknown civilization that date back 350,000 years. Thousands of years later, enormous glaciers covered Switzerland and destroyed all plant and animal life. From time to time, the glaciers partially retreated, allowing roaming bands of hunters to pass through the Jura Mountains and the Mittelland.

By the thirteenth century B.C., the glaciers had mostly melted, and people began to resettle the area. Small communities developed on the shores of Lake Zurich and other Swiss lakes. Families cultivated plants, raised domestic animals, hunted wild game, and fished in the rivers and lakes. Later peoples created weapons, such as stone battle-axes, and made jewelry crafted from copper and tin.

By around 500 B.C., a Celtic civilization had established itself in the area. One of the Celtic settlements, known as La Tène, became an important center at Lake

Neuchâtel. The Celtic settlers, known as Helvetians, had an elaborate religion, practiced complex social customs, and made intricate artworks of metal. From this region, which became known as Helvetia, Celtic culture spread throughout much of Europe.

As the Celts came to dominate western and central Switzerland, a people known as the Rhaetians established themselves in a remote area to the east. The Rhaetians, a strong, warlike people, maintained a distance from other civilizations in central Europe.

Roman Empire

In 58 B.C., the Helvetians began to push westward, probably in search of riches in Gaul (modern France). An army from Rome, a republic centered in Italy, attacked the traveling Helvetians and then seized Helvetia. Led by their commander, Julius Caesar, the Romans were expanding from their base on the Italian Peninsula in southern Europe by conquering peoples in other parts of the continent. In fact, by 15 B.C., the Romans had captured Rhaetia as well.

The Romans granted Helvetia independence within the Roman Empire. The conquerors also gave Helvetia protection from outside attack in exchange for soldiers to strengthen the Roman army. As part of the empire, Helvetia prospered. Farms produced livestock, cereal, fruit, and wine. New roads brought increased trade, and small market towns grew more populous.

The period of peace lasted until A.D. 253, when an alliance of Germanic tribes called the Alemanni attacked Helvetian settlements from their homelands north of the Rhine River. Armies of the Roman Empire battled the Alemanni and eventually

Photo by North Wind Picture Archives

The Helvetians—a Celtic tribe centered in Switzerland—made plans to move west into Gaul (modern France) in the first century B.C. About 400,000 Helvetians set off on the trip, only to be beaten in battle by a Roman army. Fewer than 200,000 Helvetians lived to return to Switzerland following the defeat.

This Roman mosaic of a battle scene comes from Augst, a town in northern Switzerland originally founded by the Romans in the first century A.D.

regained control of Helvetia. To cover the costs of the war, however, Roman officials charged high taxes and forced the Helvetians to work without pay.

Germanic Rule

In the fourth century, other Germanic armies attacked Rome itself, forcing the Roman soldiers to abandon Helvetia to defend the Italian Peninsula. With the Romans gone, the Alemanni crossed the Rhine River and took control of Helvetia. Over the centuries, the Alemanni pushed southward, forcing many Celts into the Alps.

Meanwhile, another Germanic tribe, the Burgundians, moved into what is now the French-speaking region of western Switzerland. Unlike the Alemanni, the Burgundians lived in harmony with the Celts. The two Germanic groups, which spoke separate languages and came from different parts of central Europe, maintained an uneasy peace.

A third Germanic tribe, the Franks, invaded the Swiss region in the fifth and sixth centuries A.D. The Franks conquered the territories of both the Burgundians and the Alemanni, assuming control over eastern France and much of what is now Switzerland. The Merovingians, a Frankish dynasty (family of rulers), held power in the region for the next 250 years and introduced the people to Christianity, a religion that had originated in the Middle East. A later Frankish dynasty, the Carolingians, took over the Frankish territory, including Switzerland, in the late 700s.

Holy Roman Empire

Under the Franks, people in the region gradually became Christians and members of the Roman Catholic Church. The pope, the leader of this Christian church, had his headquarters in Rome. By the ninth century, the Carolingian ruler Charlemagne reigned over a vast Christian territory, including modern-day Switzerland, France, the Netherlands, Austria, Italy, and nearly all of eastern Europe. Even the pope recognized Charlemagne's power by crowning him emperor of the Holy Roman Empire in A.D. 800.

Under Charlemagne and his successors, nobles in Switzerland and throughout Europe owned huge tracts of land and hired private armies to protect them against outside enemies. Each noble controlled a small piece of the Carolingian realm but owed loyalty to the emperor. Authority passed from generation to generation, as did the nobles' allegiance to the empire.

Beneath the nobles was a hierarchy of stewards, artisans, and landless peasants. Called serfs, the peasants worked for the nobles without pay in return for food and protection, and were forbidden to leave the estates to which they were legally bound. Small-scale landowners also turned over part of their harvest to nobles in return for protection. This political and social system, called feudalism, lasted for several hundred years.

The Swiss Confederation

During the eleventh century, powerful nobles within the Holy Roman Empire disputed the authority of the emperor. The empire began losing control in the Swiss region, allowing feudal dynasties to gain

Photo by Janet Bennett

Chillon Castle on Lake Geneva was built between the eleventh and thirteenth centuries for the nobles of the Savoy family.

Photo by Drs. A. A. M. van der Heyden, Naarden, the Netherlands

Successive emperors of the Holy Roman Empire wore this crown for 900 years. The Habsburg dynasty (family of rulers) governed the empire beginning in 1273.

power over large territories. Feudal lords established towns throughout the region and developed important trade links with merchants in many parts of Europe. Villagers used roads to bring their livestock to market towns, where the animals were traded for grains from farming areas in Switzerland and Italy.

By the thirteenth century, the Savoy, Zahringen, Kyburg, and Habsburg dynasties controlled much of Switzerland. The Habsburgs, a family that originated near Zurich, eventually became the most powerful dynasty and expanded its borders to include more and more territory.

In 1273 Rudolf I became the first Habsburg to rule as emperor of the Holy Roman Empire. Meanwhile, large numbers of peasants fled the feudal estates or bought their freedom with money earned from selling their food products. Free from the control of nobles, these peasants populated the rural cantons (districts) of Schwyz,

Uri, and Unterwalden in central Switzerland. After assuming power of the Holy Roman Empire, the Habsburgs began to intrude upon these communities.

In 1291 the leaders of Schwyz, Uri, and Unterwalden made a pact. Intent on forming a separate country, the group agreed that an attack on any member would be considered an attack on all. The leaders also agreed to resolve their own disputes and to resist outside interference.

The pact marked the beginning of the Swiss Confederation. The confederation formed a democratic union and set up a legislative policy called the Landsgemeinde, in which communities met once a year to vote. The men in each community voted to elect representatives and to decide on matters of peace and war. The population of the confederation consisted mainly of farmers and villagers, because the Habsburgs held sway in the larger cities within the three cantons' borders. Habsburg-ruled regions outside the confederation watched the cantons' progress in fending off Habsburg rule.

An engraving gives an idealized view of the founding of the Swiss Confederation. Werner Stauffacher from Schwyz, Walter Fürst from Uri, and Arnold von Melchthal from Unterwalden pledged to join their cantons together as a confederation in 1291.

A well-known Swiss legend recounts the story of William Tell, a Swiss sharpshooter of the 1300s. When Tell refused to bow before the hat of an Austrian jailer, the jailer arrested him. The jailer then promised to free Tell if the Swiss patriot could shoot an apple off Tell's son's head with a crossbow. Tell succeeded and told the jailer that if he had missed, he would have killed the Austrian. The jailer again arrested Tell. While being escorted to prison, Tell escaped and shot an arrow through the jailer's heart. The incident was said to cause a large-scale revolt among the Swiss.

War and Expansion

In the 1300s, the Habsburgs—who had conquered Austria and had made it their new home—mounted a campaign against the founding cantons. The Habsburg's goal was to take control of St. Gotthard Pass, a major route through the Alps in southern Uri. During the Battle of Morgarten in Schwyz in 1315, confederation troops defeated the Habsburg armies.

By the late fourteenth century, the Swiss Confederation had expanded to include the cantons of Bern, Lucerne, Zug, Zurich, and Glarus. The growing confederation produced a strong military force, defeating the Habsburg armies in 1386 and again in 1388. The confederation's army also won several important battles against other European forces to gain land.

During this century of the confederation's growth, canton leaders agreed for the most part on how to share power. By the mid-1400s, however, Zurich tried to absorb territory east and south of its borders. To achieve its goals, Zurich renewed an alliance with the Austrian Habsburgs. This move caused the confederation's army to react. By 1450, after several bitter battles, Zurich admitted defeat, severing its alliance with the Habsburgs and rejoining the Swiss Confederation.

In the late 1400s and the early 1500s, the confederation engaged in three major conflicts. In the 1470s, the Swiss battled

Ticino became part of the Swiss Confederation in the early 1500s.

Burgundy, a duchy (duke's territory) that covered northeastern France. With help from the Austrians and from the French, the Swiss defeated the Burgundians. As a result of the war, Fribourg and Solothurn, two regions that had allied with the Swiss during the conflict, became new cantons in the Swiss Confederation in 1481.

In the 1490s, the Austrian emperor Maximilian I attempted to reestablish control over the Holy Roman Empire, which still—at least in name—included the Swiss Confederation. After the Austrian armies attacked Graubünden, a region to the east of the confederation, the Swiss fought back. The Swiss defeated the Austrian army and retained their unofficial independence from the empire.

Early in the 1500s, the Swiss were drawn into a struggle over the Po Valley, a large fertile plain in northern Italy. The struggle included Austria, France, and Italy. In 1515 French forces defeated the Swiss, who lost more than 8,000 troops. The peace treaty that followed the war left the Swiss with Ticino, a chunk of territory to the south of the confederation. The treaty also established a free-trade system between Switzerland and France, giving the Swiss access to a larger foreign market.

Swiss industries grew, as more peasants moved from the countryside to cities and towns to manufacture textiles, glassware, and wooden and metal goods. Skilled Swiss soldiers were another important export. Many of them left to fight for France, a nation that wanted more troops to expand its military power.

The Protestant Reformation

Economic shifts in Switzerland and throughout Europe during the 1400s and 1500s were coupled with social and religious changes. For centuries the Swiss and most other Europeans had been loyal Roman Catholics. But over time some members of the Roman Catholic clergy had grown rich and corrupt and were vying among themselves for power. Meanwhile, other religious leaders protested the corruption, calling for changes in the way the church was run. Their demands were the beginnings of the Protestant Reformation.

Within the Swiss Confederation, the foremost supporter of religious reform was a Catholic priest from Zurich named Huldreich Zwingli. Along with reformers in Germany and France, Zwingli wanted to move the Roman Catholic Church away from lavish ceremonies and toward a simpler form of worship based on readings of the Bible.

Zwingli's Protestant philosophy soon took hold in other German-speaking Swiss cities. But many Catholics, especially those living in rural areas, were frightened by Zwingli and by what they saw as an

Bern's Gothic cathedral, begun in the fifteenth century, was converted during the Reformation from a Catholic to a Protestant church.

Photo © Don Eastman

25

assault on their faith. The division caused the Swiss Catholics and the Swiss Protestants to resort to violence to resolve their differences.

In 1531 Zwingli and his supporters fought against an army from the rural Catholic cantons—Uri, Schwyz, Unterwalden, Glarus, Zug, and Appenzell—at the Battle of Kappel in Zurich canton. Zwingli was killed, but the ensuing peace agreement allowed the Swiss to practice whatever religion they pleased.

After Zwingli's death, another Protestant reformer, the Frenchman John Calvin, moved to Geneva to further develop his own religious doctrines. Calvin believed in the close cooperation of the church and government. Eventually, Geneva's leaders offered Calvin a chance to put his ideas into practice.

An ambitious reformer with a flair for administration, Calvin reorganized Geneva's civil and religious government. The city's decision-making power would be in the hands of a nonreligious council, which would be expected to rule according to the teachings of Geneva's reformed church. Under the church's influence, city leaders passed laws that banned card playing, backgammon, drinking alcohol, and other activities that Calvin considered sinful. Calvin also founded a religious academy that later became the University of Geneva.

Independence and Growth

Surviving the religious and social changes of the 1500s strengthened the identity of the Swiss Confederation, which had 13 members by the end of the sixteenth century. While struggles between Protestants and Catholics in other European countries led to the Thirty Years' War (1618–1648), Switzerland chose to remain neutral. After the war, a treaty called the Peace of Westphalia officially recognized Switzerland as an independent and neutral nation.

Swiss leaders set up a loose national government, in which each of the cantons

Huldreich Zwingli read Christian scriptures in their original languages to better interpret the teachings. He and his followers quit worshiping Catholic saints, rid their churches of ornaments, and stopped following the rules of the Roman Catholic faith.

John Calvin taught his reformed religion in the 1530s. After establishing Protestantism in Geneva, Calvin spread his religious ideals to France.

sent two representatives to a general assembly called the Diet. Because the Diet met infrequently and was designed to have little authority, local governing bodies continued to make all the important decisions. Moreover, the confederation split along religious lines between Roman Catholic and Protestant cantons.

Switzerland's rural cantons, where most people practiced the Catholic faith, relied on the Landsgemeinde to make laws. In the mainly Protestant urban cantons of Bern, Fribourg, Solothurn, and Lucerne, wealthy landowning families controlled the local governments. The same type of political system operated in Zurich, Basel, and Schaffhausen but under rich families that had made their money from trade instead of from agriculture. The lack of national unity caused tensions, but the Swiss maintained an uneasy peace and spent their energies developing textile and watchmaking industries.

By the eighteenth century, Switzerland was prospering. Peasants raised dairy cows for milk and grew crops, selling the foodstuffs to processors in the towns. The peasants also herded sheep, whose wool supplied the confederation's busy cloth-weaving mills. By the late 1700s, the textile industries in Zurich, Glarus, and Basel were booming. In Geneva and in the Jura Mountains, small watch- and clock-making industries had grown into an international business.

French Occupation

This period of economic expansion could not hide increasing social tensions within Switzerland. Migrations of peasants to the cities caused great unrest in Geneva, Bern, and Lucerne as their populations grew. The wealthy ruling elite in these cities refused to yield power to the expanding number of burghers, or free townspeople, who objected to paying taxes without also having the right to vote. At the same time, religious skirmishes occasionally erupted between Catholics and Protestants.

Meanwhile, unrest in France led to the French Revolution, an event that affected all of Europe and especially Switzerland. In 1798, after republican (anti-monarchy) leaders ousted the French king, an army under the French commander Napoleon

Workers in an eighteenth-century cheesemaker's shop process cheeses from Switzerland's plentiful supply of milk. The milk is left until the whey (liquid) separates from the curd (solid). The worker in the foreground presses still more whey from the curds of cheese. The curds are then formed into large chunks, set aside to drain more whey, and finally packed in molds to age.

Bonaparte invaded Switzerland. Napoleon abolished the system of cantons, imposed a new central government, and renamed the country the Helvetic Republic.

French officials wrote a new Swiss constitution, which abolished the power and privileges of the Swiss aristocracy. This change further eroded the power of the old feudal and merchant families that had dominated the urban cantons. Many Swiss supported the new constitution but strongly opposed the French occupation of their country. As outsiders, the French leaders

had difficulty creating a uniform national government in a country with major ethnic, religious, and cultural divisions.

To stabilize the situation, Napoleon asked Swiss representatives to come to Paris in 1803 to sign the Act of Mediation, which reformed the constitution. The act created a federalist system that granted individual cantons authority over local issues. The Swiss federal government, on the other hand, would have power in areas of international relations, military matters, currency regulations, and war and peace. In addition, the act carved 6 new cantons out of the existing ones, forming a total of 19 cantons. The act also guaranteed that citizens would be treated equally before the law, a move that ended feudalism for good in Switzerland.

In return for these reforms, the Swiss agreed to allow France to draft Swiss soldiers into its army. The constitution, however, only lasted as long as Napoleon's reign, which ended in 1815, after the Great Powers—a coalition of European armies—defeated him.

Constitutional Reform

In 1815, at the Congress of Vienna, the four Great Powers (Russia, Britain, Prussia, and Austria) determined the future of regions formerly held by Napoleon. The agreement created three new Swiss cantons, all of which had been ancient allies of the confederation. Geneva, Valais, and Neuchâtel brought the total number of cantons to 22. The postwar agreement also recognized Switzerland as a permanently neutral and independent country in Europe.

One issue not addressed at the Congress of Vienna was the Swiss constitution. The fall of Napoleon had dissolved

By 1812 French commander Napoleon Bonaparte controlled territory that stretched eastward from Spain to Poland and southward from Norway to Italy.

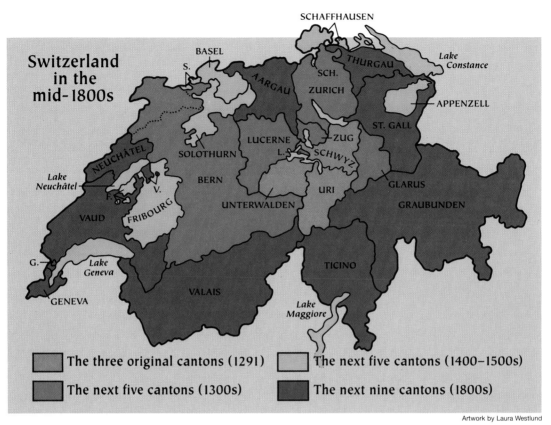

Switzerland in the mid-1800s

SCHAFFHAUSEN

BASEL
S.
AARGAU
THURGAU
SCH.
ZURICH
Lake Constance
APPENZELL
ST. GALL
LUCERNE
ZUG
SCHWYZ
NEUCHÂTEL
SOLOTHURN
L. S.
Lake Neuchâtel
BERN
V.
F.
URI
GLARUS
GRAUBUNDEN
VAUD
FRIBOURG
G.
Lake Geneva
UNTERWALDEN
GENEVA
VALAIS
TICINO
Lake Maggiore

☐ The three original cantons (1291)   ☐ The next five cantons (1400–1500s)
☐ The next five cantons (1300s)   ☐ The next nine cantons (1800s)

Artwork by Laura Westlund

By the mid-1800s, Switzerland had 22 cantons. The only future change occurred in 1979, when Jura canton *(dotted line)* was carved from northwestern Bern.

the constitution, returning Switzerland to a loosely knit group of semi-independent cantons controlled largely by a few powerful families. Religious and social tensions flared again, as workers and peasants pushed for a more democratic Swiss government. As the reform movement gained strength in the 1830s, governments in several cantons were overthrown.

In 1834 citizens of the most urban and liberal cantons pushed for a tax on church property, for freedom of worship, and for a secular (nonreligious) public school system. This campaign upset residents of the seven conservative Catholic cantons, which formed a group to oppose the measures. Called the Sonderbund, the group refused the federal government's demand to disband, leading to a three-week civil war in 1847. The Sonderbund's army was

destroyed, and the next year Switzerland again rewrote its constitution.

THE 1848 CONSTITUTION

The constitution written in 1848 carefully weighed the division of power between the cantons and the federal government. To ensure its neutrality in any future European conflicts, Switzerland made provisions for an army and a defense system to prevent enemy attacks. In addition, the constitution set up a uniform standard of customs, measures, and currency to make business transactions more efficient.

The new constitution resolved Switzerland's most troublesome political problems, allowing the country to focus on economic activities. As a result, the economy took off in the mid-1800s. Foreign trade increased and industrial development expanded, in

29

Beginning in the early 1900s, tourism played a big part in Switzerland's economy. Here, vacationers visit Gstaad, a ski resort in the Swiss Alps, in 1934.

part because of the country's free-trade policy. Switzerland did not charge tariffs (taxes) on goods imported from other nations as long as its trading partners allowed Swiss exports to be sold tax free in their countries. This free-trade policy provided the small nation with plenty of foreign markets for its goods.

Largely unburdened by governmental restrictions, Swiss businesses grew quickly. A well-educated class of businesspeople and government officials helped Switzerland adapt to changing trends in industrial and world markets. The Swiss built extensive rail and road systems to transport their products, used machines to increase productivity, and negotiated favorable trade agreements with other nations. Even tourism played a role in the nation's prosperity, as vacationers and health-spa visitors alike traveled to Switzerland to enjoy its pure and healthy Alpine air.

Guarding Swiss Neutrality

Europe in the 1900s was the scene of two world wars. Although Switzerland remained neutral during both World War I (1914–1918) and World War II (1939–1945), the country became a place of refuge for exiles and offered medical help to victims of war through the International Red Cross. During World War I, a conflict that pitted France against Germany, Switzerland suffered some tension between its German-speaking and French-speaking citizens. In addition, the danger of being drawn into the war remained strong throughout the conflict.

Switzerland also experienced economic problems during the war. Swiss companies had difficulty importing the raw materials needed for manufacturing. Nor could these firms sell many products to the European nations at war. The government enlisted farmers and workers to guard the country against attack, a change that brought food and labor into short supply.

After the war, which France and its allies won, Switzerland joined the League of Nations, an organization formed in 1920 to prevent future wars. Switzerland remained neutral within the organization and offered it a base in Geneva. The country's neutral status proved hard to maintain, however. For example, league members imposed economic sanctions (punishments) on nations they deemed dangerous and used a multinational army to stop disturbances.

Neutrality became even more difficult in 1935, when Italy—under Benito Mussolini—invaded the African nation of Ethiopia. The League of Nations imposed an economic boycott on Italy. Like other league members, Switzerland refused to sell arms to Italy but would not agree to stop trading other goods. The Swiss saw this as a proper neutral policy, but other league members strongly opposed it.

Mussolini, a powerful leader who supported fascism—a form of government with one all-powerful ruler and no legislature—had plans to expand his empire in other directions as well. Similarly, Adolf Hitler, Germany's fascist head of state, aimed to conquer outside territories. By the late 1930s, these two leaders had formed a coalition called the Axis. World War II erupted in 1939, when Hitler's armies invaded Poland, causing Britain and France to declare war on Germany.

The Swiss had prepared for the conflict by mobilizing 850,000 soldiers—almost one

Swiss soldiers on border patrol during World War II (1939–1945) paused for a quick meal.

out of every four citizens—to defend the small nation's borders. Workers sped up production of staple goods and stored food and fuel to prevent wartime shortages.

At the same time, Swiss bankers gave secret bank accounts to German and Italian Jews who were victims of fascist persecution. Several Swiss businesspeople helped operate secret networks to move Jewish people safely out of Germany and Italy. Switzerland also attracted wartime spies, who served either the pro-fascist Axis powers or their opponents, the Allied powers. This group included France, Great Britain, the United States, and the Soviet Union.

The wartime years were difficult for the Swiss, despite their neutral stance. The Axis powers, controlled by Germany's Nazi party, surrounded Switzerland. The Swiss rationed food, froze prices, and accepted thousands of refugees. As a neutral country, Switzerland traded with the Axis powers until 1944, when pressure from the Allies forced it to stop. In 1945 the Allies defeated the Nazi forces, effectively ending the war in Europe.

Postwar Developments

Unlike much of the rest of Europe, Switzerland escaped World War II with little damage. The sound Swiss economy enabled Swiss companies to provide European nations with loans and with consumer goods to help reconstruction efforts.

Courtesy of National Archives

When freed from prison camps at the end of World War II, Jewish refugees such as this young boy were transported to safety in Switzerland.

Independent Picture Service

During the 1950s and 1960s, businesses grew rapidly in Switzerland. Workers busily packaged chocolates *(left)* and assembled watches *(below)*.

Independent Picture Service

Switzerland's neutrality again became an issue in the postwar years. The Allies pressured Switzerland to join the United Nations (UN), an international diplomatic organization that established its European offices in the former League of Nations building in Geneva. The Swiss declined to join but did become an active member of several UN agencies, such as the World Health Organization and the Food and Agriculture Organization.

During the 1950s, the Swiss economy grew rapidly. The manufacturing and service sectors boomed with the help of a well-trained workforce and a lack of labor disputes. Swiss businesses produced specialized, high-quality goods for the global market. By making large investments in research, Swiss corporations joined the world's leading manufacturers of chemicals and high-tech products. Banking and finance also developed at a fast pace. Economic growth attracted rural residents to cities and suburbs, where new jobs were available. Because of industrial expansion,

the wages of Swiss workers rose 250 percent during the 1950s and 1960s.

Economic development had other effects. With nearly full employment, Swiss companies began to hire foreign workers. From the 1950s to the 1970s, Switzerland welcomed more than one million foreigners, who eventually composed 17 percent of the population. These immigrants accounted for half of the population growth in Switzerland during this time period.

An international oil crisis in the early 1970s slowed the Swiss economy. Businesses had to pay skyrocketing prices to fuel their factories, and many were forced to close. Inflation soared, and 7 percent of the workforce lost their jobs. For the first time in decades, Switzerland experienced labor unrest, as Swiss workers demanded that businesses break their contracts with 200,000 foreign employees.

Although Switzerland's style of government had smoothed over most ethnic tensions by the 1970s, some problems still arose. By the end of the decade, the creation of the new canton of Jura addressed social problems in northwestern Switzerland. Carved from the canton of Bern, Jura

became the twenty-third canton in 1979. The division gave the primarily French-speaking Catholic population of Jura independence from Bern, which was made up of mainly German-speaking Protestants.

A constitutional amendment in 1981 guaranteed equal rights for Swiss women. The amendment ended the discrimination women had faced at work and in educational settings. The amendment also forced cantons and communities that did not allow women to vote to change their laws.

Recent Events

Environmental issues and health concerns surfaced in Switzerland in the 1980s and

Demonstrators in Zurich protest the closing of "Needle Park," an area in the city popular among drug addicts. In the mid-1990s, city officials cracked down on drug use in the park to combat rising crime and health risks.

Photo by Reuters/Bettmann

After 30 tons of chemicals spilled into the Rhine River at Basel in 1986, workers scooped out load after load of dead eels and other fish killed by the toxic materials.

Photo by DPA

The Swiss flag, featuring a white cross on a red background, is said to have been first used on a battlefield in 1339. The flag was officially adopted in 1848.

Artwork by Laura Westlund

1990s. Many Swiss organized to promote antipollution laws and to protest certain types of development, such as expanding the country's nuclear energy production. The Swiss also faced a rising number of cases of AIDS (acquired immune deficiency syndrome) during the 1980s, when Switzerland recorded the most new cases of AIDS of any European country. Many of the infected people were drug users who shared dirty needles.

Immigration again became a controversial topic in the 1980s, when about 50,000 foreigners came to Switzerland seeking political asylum (protection). Immigration policies in Switzerland drew much debate, with some Swiss arguing to keep all immigrants out of the country. The fear of some citizens that immigrants would cause rising unemployment and overcrowding prompted the government to tighten immigration and asylum policies. Nonetheless, Switzerland still welcomed refugees much more willingly than did most other European nations.

Meanwhile, the international community pressured Swiss bankers and politicians to ease the nation's bank secrecy laws, which allowed suspected criminals to conceal their wealth in Swiss banks. Although Switzerland upheld the legality of its historically secret bank accounts, Swiss banking officials agreed to share records on alleged criminals with outside investigators on a special-permission basis.

In the 1990s, the Swiss debated whether to join the European Union (EU), an organization of European nations in a free-market alliance. Many Swiss believed that by joining the EU the country would compromise its longstanding traditions of neutrality and independence. Others felt that by not joining, the Swiss would lose influence in European affairs and would be hurt economically.

In 1992 voters in a national referendum (public vote) decided that Switzerland would not became part of the European Economic Area, a free-trade zone associated with the EU. The Swiss likely will continue to debate their relations with the EU through the end of the century. Despite its problems, Switzerland's strong economy and healthy democracy have prepared the country to face the future with confidence.

Government

Switzerland is a federal republic, with powers divided between the national and

The 200 members of the national council assemble in the Bundeshaus in Bern. Elected for four-year terms, council members meet four times per year for three-week sessions.

cantonal governments. The federal government has a president, an executive federal council, and a two-house federal assembly. One chamber of the federal assembly—the national council—has 200 members, each of whom serve four-year

A young man readies his gear for a period of military training. Swiss males between the ages of 20 and 50 must be ready for possible military duty.

terms. The members of the national council are elected through a system of proportional representation, in which each political party receives a percentage of seats based on the percentage of votes the party receives in national elections.

The other chamber of the federal assembly, the council of states, has 46 representatives directly elected from the country's 23 cantons, 3 of which are divided into half-cantons. The six half-cantons have only one representative each in the council of states, while full cantons each send two.

The federal assembly elects seven cabinet members to serve four-year terms in the nation's federal council. These officials lead six ministries that form the executive branch of the government. Each year the federal assembly chooses one member of the federal council to serve as Switzerland's president for a one-year term. The Swiss president's position is largely ceremonial.

The Swiss rely on the popular referendum, in which the people make decisions on issues through a direct vote. The Swiss also use initiative measures, through which they may challenge a federal law or ask for new laws. The Swiss federal court, called the federal tribunal, is located in Lausanne. Generally, the court reviews cases involving lawsuits between cantons or corporations. Unlike most supreme courts, the Swiss tribunal does not review federal legislation. Every canton has its own court system.

Switzerland's cantons each have their own constitutions, parliaments, courts, and administrations. Some cantons use the Landsgemeinde—the traditional Swiss open-air popular assembly where citizens vote on issues by a show of hands. The same type of open-air assembly operates in many small villages and towns. The 23 cantons are divided into 3,000 communes, which serve as local political units.

Women in Glarus participated in a Landsgemeinde (open-air vote) in 1972, just one year after Swiss women had been granted the right to vote.

Two young men show off their flag-throwing skills during a folk festival in the Swiss Alps.

3) The People

Switzerland is one of the most ethnically and linguistically diverse nations in Europe. Although most Swiss citizens have French, German, or Italian backgrounds, the Swiss identity has remained intact for centuries. Of the total population of 7 million, about 1 million people were born outside the country. Most immigrants have come from other parts of Europe, including Spain, Italy, Germany, and France.

The country's overall population density is 459 people per square mile, but in reality, some Alpine areas are sparsely populated. More than two-thirds of the Swiss population live in urban areas. The metropolitan areas of Zurich, Basel, Geneva, Bern, Lausanne, Lucerne, and St. Gall each have more than 100,000 people. The cantons of Zurich and Bern have the most residents.

Ethnic Groups and Languages

The original Swiss population descended mainly from French and German peoples who conquered the region in the fifth century A.D. The Italian-speaking cantons became part of Switzerland much later. Over time, as the population intermarried and moved around, the linguistic borders blurred. Yet small ethnic pockets survived among the larger French-, German-, and Italian-speaking regions. A fourth ethnic group in eastern Switzerland descended from the ancient Rhaetian peoples. These people speak Romansh, a language closely related to Latin.

Switzerland maintains three official languages—German, French, and Italian. About 65 percent of the population speak mostly German, 18 percent use French, and nearly 10 percent speak Italian. Although not official, Romansh is a national language used by about 1 percent of the Swiss population, chiefly in the eastern

Photo © Don Eastman

Revelers don bright costumes for the Fastnacht carnival in Saas-Fee, Switzerland. This festival is held the week before Lent, a springtime Christian religious observance.

Photo © Jeff Strong/Photo Agora

A Mennonite family relaxes outside its home in Moron, Switzerland. The Mennonites, a religious group that originated in Zurich during the Reformation, believe in a simple way of life based on the teachings of the Christian Bible.

Swiss Alps. Most Swiss are fluent in more than one language.

German-speakers make up the largest group in 16 of the northern and central cantons, among them Zurich and Bern. In these places, most Swiss use a form of German called Schwyzerdütsch (also known as Baseldütsch in Basel and Zuridütsch in Zurich). Spoken Schwyzerdütsch, or Swiss German, differs greatly from standard German, which appears in all written materials where Swiss German is spoken. Even within Swiss German regions, several different dialects of the language exist.

The predominantly French-speaking area of Switzerland covers mainly the western cantons of Geneva, Neuchâtel, Jura, Vaud, and parts of Fribourg and Valais. The French spoken in these regions is very similar to the traditional language of France. Many of the customs and traditions of the French-speaking Swiss also resemble those of their French neighbors. The Italian-speaking region of southern Switzerland includes Lugano and Locarno, the largest Italian-speaking cities.

Religion

Switzerland is a mostly Christian nation, almost equally divided between Roman Catholics and Protestants. Catholics and Protestants often live in the same cantons, although one group or the other usually forms a majority. As a result of Switzerland's ever-increasing diversity, religions new to the country have also found a home. In larger cities, houses of worship exist for people of Jewish, Islamic, Greek Orthodox, and other faiths.

Although Switzerland has no national religion, a canton may designate one or

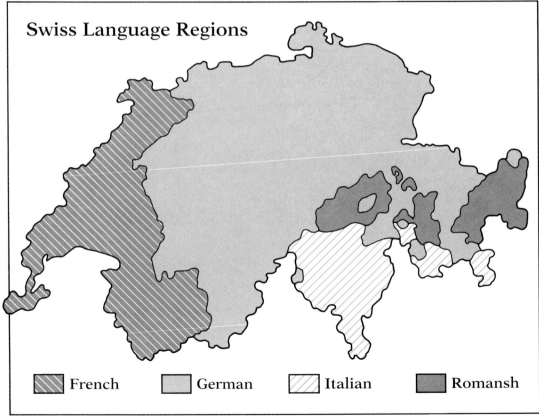

Swiss Language Regions

French German Italian Romansh

Artwork by Laura Westlund

Swiss students receive a diverse education, which includes hands-on subjects such as metalworking *(left)*. At the forefront of Swiss educational development was Johann Pestalozzi *(below)*, who believed schooling should encompass a wide range of activities to help students master practical skills.

more denominations as official churches. This policy allows a church to receive tax money from the cantonal government for its expenses. Citizens, however, may withhold taxes used for this purpose. The nation has long been sensitive to religious influences on government. For example, the Swiss constitution prohibits any clergy member from serving on the national council. The creation of new religious orders, convents, or districts without federal consent is also against the law.

Education

Switzerland has long had one of the world's best educational systems, for which the Swiss often credit Johann Pestalozzi (1746–1827), an influential Swiss educator. In the late 1700s, Pestalozzi developed a new method for teaching children. He believed that education began in the home and that the family provided a child with

Schoolchildren in Täsch, a town in the Swiss Alps, take a break from studying. Most Swiss master at least two languages by the time they complete school.

the most basic and important lessons. School, Pestalozzi felt, should model the elements of family learning by teaching children practical skills, ethics, and sensitivity to the physical world. Pestalozzi advocated a type of instruction that used concrete, hands-on situations to introduce concepts. He also pushed for education to be made available to every child.

The cantons control the school systems in their regions with little oversight from the federal government. The dominant

Students compare grades at a school crossing. The grading system in Switzerland ranges from one to four—a one being equivalent to an A in the U.S. school system.

Courtesy of Swiss National Tourist Office

The University of Zurich is Switzerland's largest institution of higher learning. About 16,000 students attend the school each year.

language in each canton is the language taught in public schools. Students attend small classes and study a demanding curriculum. The Swiss education system has led the way to a literacy rate of 99 percent.

Primary and secondary school attendance is mandatory in Switzerland, but because school policy varies from canton to canton, the ages of the students at each level fluctuate. In most cantons, primary school includes grades one through six, and secondary school encompasses grades seven through nine. After completing secondary school, students may go on to high school, where they focus on one of three specialties—Greek and Latin, modern languages, or math and science. Students may instead take a Lehre, or apprenticeship, during which they learn a trade while attending a technical or vocational school.

Students who complete high school can attend one of Switzerland's public colleges, which charge no tuition to citizens. About 15 percent of Swiss students attend universities. The largest are those in Basel, Zurich, Bern, Geneva, Lausanne, Fribourg, St. Gall, and Neuchâtel. Another

Photo © Luke Golobitsh

Scholars at the University of Bern discuss a class project. About 30,000 students attend Switzerland's nine universities.

Youngsters run and climb at a playground in Zurich. With a low birthrate and a low death rate, Switzerland has a very slow-growing population. About 15 percent of the population is under the age of 15. At current rates of growth, the Swiss population will not double for more than 200 years.

college, the Federal Institute of Technology in Zurich, has produced more Nobel Prize winners than any other center of scientific learning in the world.

Health

The Swiss government funds a health-care system that offers free or low-cost medical services for sickness, childbirth, and tem-

porary disability. The nation's clinics and hospitals are well staffed and equipped with modern technologies. The infant mortality rate in Switzerland is low at 6 deaths per every 1,000 live births. Life expectancy for the Swiss is 78 years, one of the highest in the world.

Although the Swiss enjoy relatively high health standards, concern over drug abuse and the spread of AIDS is growing. The number of AIDS patients in Switzerland is on the rise, partly because of the large number of drug addicts who share needles. Switzerland has one of the highest rates of heroin addiction in Europe. Between 10,000 and 15,000 homeless drug addicts live in the nation.

The Arts

The diversity of languages and cultures in Switzerland has hampered the creation of a true national culture. Yet the country's neutrality has made it a haven for foreign artists and writers seeking a safe place to work. Over the centuries, many world-famous poets, writers, artists, and musicians have moved to Switzerland to escape unrest and persecution in their homelands.

At the same time, many Swiss authors have moved to France or to Germany for inspiration, and their literary subjects often reflect events in those two countries. Switzerland's two most famous books are adventure tales for young people—Johann Wyss's *Swiss Family Robinson* and Johanna Spyri's *Heidi.* The author of *Heidi* portrays the beauty and healing powers of the Swiss Alps in a story about a girl, her grandfather, and an ill friend she nurses back to health in the clean mountain air.

Independent Picture Service

Johanna Spyri (1827–1901), the author of *Heidi,* was born and raised near Zurich. Spyri wrote the well-known story for her son, drawing from her own childhood to create the settings and characters.

Wyss's novel tells the story of a family stranded on an island, where four young brothers learn teamwork in the wilderness.

Many Swiss authors—including Jakob Burckhardt, Conrad Meyer, Gottfried Keller, Hermann Hesse, and Carl Spitteler—treat philosophical concepts in their works. Friedrich Dürrenmatt and Max

Independent Picture Service

Delicate Swiss ceramics made in the mid-1700s stand on display in Zurich.

45

Frisch, two German-language playwrights, have received praise for their works, which focus on human character and morality.

Several Swiss artists found fame in the twentieth century. The painter Paul Klee created colorful, abstract canvases and drawings. Alberto Giacometti, an internationally renowned Swiss sculptor, worked in Paris during much of his lifetime. His long, sticklike figures appear to be frozen in motion.

The Swiss have not been at the forefront of musical life in Europe, but a few talented composers have emerged. Arthur Honegger, one of Switzerland's leading composers, worked with a group of French musicians called Les Six. He is known for *Pacific 231, Judith,* and *Antigone.* Other notable Swiss musicians include composer Frank Martin, pianist Edwin Fischer, and conductor Ernest Ansermet, who in 1918 founded L'Orchestre de la Suisse Romande in Geneva.

Recreation and Sports

The rugged landscape of the Swiss Alps allows a wide variety of outdoor sports, including downhill and cross-country skiing, two of the most popular activities. About 40 percent of the population ski regularly, and ski trails can be found near most cities and villages. Ski enthusiasts travel from all over the world to test themselves against Switzerland's steep and challenging slopes.

Independent Picture Service

The Swiss sculptor Alberto Giacometti (1901–1966) created this bronze figure of a walking cat in 1955.

A musician plays an *alpenhorn*—an instrument that dates to the 1200s. Originally used as a warning signal or to call soldiers in the high mountain districts to battle, the horn can be heard as far as eight miles away.

Skiers reach the bottom of a run at Champéry, a resort in the Valais Alps.

Hornussen players *(above)* field the *hornuss*—a type of wooden ball—with large rackets called *schindels.* Curling *(right)* also attracts many Swiss players. In this sport, team members push large stones down a long lane of ice toward a target called the house.

The Swiss also enjoy bobsledding, soccer, cycling, hiking, mountain climbing, racquet sports, swimming, golf, and fishing. Target shooting has many Swiss fans, some of whom master the skill in the military. The Swiss also enjoy playing *hornussen,* a popular team game with elements of baseball and tennis.

Climbers tackle a sharp, snowy ridge on Mount Mönch (13,445 feet). Mountaineering—the sport of scaling mountains—is popular in the Swiss Alps.

A woman in Valais canton awaits a serving of *raclette,* a popular Swiss dish. Half of a cheese round is placed near a hot fire. When the edge of the cheese melts, it is scraped off and eaten with potatoes and onions.

Food

Like its culture and ethnic makeup, Switzerland has a cuisine that varies from canton to canton. In most places, Italian, German, and French dishes are common. Ethnic restaurants in large cities also serve foods from around the world.

Swiss cooking can be divided into two types—haute, or high, cuisine and traditional cuisine. Haute cuisine is more common in wealthy homes and sophisticated urban restaurants. Traditional fare includes the everyday and festival foods of most Swiss families.

In the Swiss Alps, rich milk, cheese, and bread make up at least part of most meals. In southwestern Switzerland, French cuisine is popular, with wine stews, organ meats, beef, sausages, and rich sauces. French-speakers also favor fondue dishes, which usually feature a hot, rich cheese sauce.

In Ticino, Italian risotto, gnocchi, polenta, and mushrooms make up much of the daily fare. Cooks in the German cantons serve pork and plenty of *rösti*, a patty of hash brown potatoes flavored with bacon, herbs, and cheese. Muesli, a breakfast cereal developed by a doctor in Zurich, contains rolled oats, spelt (a grain), nuts, raisins, apples, and spices.

The Swiss usually eat a breakfast of hot chocolate or coffee, milk, bread, butter, and jam. The main meal happens at midday. In late afternoon, many people snack on pastries and other sweets. The Swiss, in fact, are known around the world for their chocolate. Evening meals in Switzerland are normally light suppers. Most Swiss meals include a salad, a bowl of soup, and a main dish. Many adults enjoy wines made by the country's productive vineyards in Valais canton and on the slopes overlooking Lakes Geneva and Neuchâtel.

Independent Picture Service

Children in Davos, in Graubünden canton, enjoy hot chocolate with whipped cream after an afternoon of sledding.

Photo by Robert L. and Diane Wolfe

Omelettes *(above)* served with a sweet fruit compote in the Romansh-language areas of Graubünden make a tasty breakfast. Poached fish with stuffed tomatoes *(right)* is a dish that combines flavors from Swiss lakes, gardens, and dairies.

Photo by Robert L. and Diane Wolfe

Photo © Luke Golobitsh

A family sits down for dinner on a farm in the Jura Mountains.

The Swiss transportation system is one of the most efficient networks in the world. The railroad lines include hundreds of tunnels and the world's highest cogwheel railway (rail system designed for mountains), which reaches the peak of Mount Jungfrau in the Bernese Alps.

4) The Economy

Switzerland's location in the middle of Europe placed it at the crossroads of many trade routes. With mountains to the north and to the south, the Mittelland served as a natural east-west link in ancient times. Early control and development of natural Alpine passes also fostered a commercial network centered in Switzerland. By the eighteenth century, improved transportation systems helped develop Switzerland's financial and manufacturing industries. The nation also began to capture tourist income, as vacationers traveled through the country's scenic landscapes.

Neutrality has been another factor in Switzerland's success. Switzerland did not fight in either World War I or World War II and has enjoyed 150 years of peace.

53

While the world wars destroyed many European economies and cities, Switzerland was able to invest in new technologies. During the first half of the century, for example, more than half of the Swiss workforce was employed in manufacturing, producing watches, electrical machinery, processed foods, and fine textiles. After World War II, the Swiss economy further expanded its banking and tourism sectors.

Switzerland has prospered without the benefit of significant natural resources or large tracts of productive farmland. Instead, the nation's economy is based on tourism, on the export of specialized manufactured goods, and on international finance. Geneva's role as headquarters for a variety of international organizations has also created employment for the Swiss labor force.

Manufacturing

Tradition suggests that the long winters in Switzerland have created a nation of skilled

Workers in a chemical plant oversee the production of a pharmaceutical drug.

The various stages in the production of a Swiss watch reveal the inner workings of the timepiece. More than 95 percent of the watches made in Switzerland are exported to other countries.

craftspeople. With many months of each year spent indoors, Swiss workers have long been able to hone their skills in making complex products. The modern Swiss economy produces machinery, construction materials, printed goods, jewelry, timepieces, chemicals, clothing, and food and beverages.

Concentrated in northern Switzerland, the manufacturing sector employs about one-half of the nation's workforce. Engineering—including the development of electronics, generators, turbines, and other high-technology products—accounts for about one-fourth of all the income from manufacturing. Many of the precision tools required to make these goods come from the country's metal industry.

Switzerland has long been known for its fine-quality clocks and watches. In recent years, this industry has consolidated and has added lower-priced watches to its traditional line of costly timepieces. The country exports nearly all of its watch production.

Switzerland operates some of Europe's largest chemical companies, which are located mainly around Basel. This industry exports more than 85 percent of its goods—including drugs, herbicides, pesticides, solvents, and fertilizers.

While the chemical business has grown, it has also come under scrutiny after a major fire occurred in a chemical warehouse near Basel in 1986. Squelching the fire caused 30 tons of toxic chemicals to wash into the Rhine River. As a result, the Swiss government passed strict environmental laws. Chemical companies have begun to modernize plants to reduce water and air pollution.

A cheesemaker loads rounds of cheese onto shelves.

The Swiss have a long-standing tradition of exporting specialized foods, including chocolates and dairy products, especially cheeses. A few large processing plants churn out substantial quantities of chocolate bars and other foodstuffs, while many smaller factories in towns and villages also make and package wines, sweets, and dairy products for export.

The manufacturing sector includes a large construction industry. Switzerland's mountainous terrain offers constant challenges to road builders and repairers. But most construction workers find jobs erecting or renovating industrial and commercial buildings.

Tourism and Trade

Tourism is vital to the Swiss economy, bringing in about $7 billion each year. Roughly 11 million people from around the world visit Switzerland for business or pleasure annually. These travelers keep Swiss workers busy in tourism-related occupations in hotels or chalets, restaurants, stores, and transportation.

In the summer months, tourists go to Switzerland's lakes, rivers, and mountains

Tourists dine outdoors at a hotel in **Scheidegg**, a resort town in the Bernese Alps.

56

The Swiss Alps offer tourists many sightseeing opportunities, including cablecar rides up to the highest peaks. This cable car excursion takes visitors to the top of Mount Schilthorn in the Bernese Alps.

to hike, relax, and sightsee. Vacationers also visit Swiss cities to tour museums, eat in fine restaurants, and shop. In winter, more than 200 ski resorts welcome about two million recreational skiers. The country also benefits from the large number of international organizations and major corporations headquartered in Geneva, Zurich, and Basel. Conventions and meetings bring in thousands of business travelers and diplomats every year.

Switzerland trades mainly with nations that belong to the European Union. Major imports include fuels, raw materials, food, and motor vehicles. The Swiss export precision engineering products, machinery, chemicals, and textiles. Switzerland's largest trading partner is Germany, which buys nearly one-fourth of all goods exported from Switzerland. German goods, in turn, represent 33 percent of Swiss imports. The nation's largest non-European trading partner is the United States.

Switzerland runs a trade deficit, meaning the country buys more goods than it sells to outsiders. But tourism and the service sector help make up the difference. Services provided to foreign businesses by Swiss banks, for example, create income from investments. When the value of financial services and tourism are taken into account, the country actually takes in more money than it pays out.

Switzerland's neutrality and its policy of bank secrecy have long attracted businesses from around the world. By law Swiss bank accounts are secret, and no government or international organization may examine banking records without special permission. More than 570 banks with 5,000 branches and loan offices are located in Switzerland.

57

Energy and Transportation

To fuel its thriving industrial sector, Switzerland depends mostly on hydroelectric power, which supplies more than 60 percent of the nation's energy needs. Two of Europe's tallest dams harness tributaries of the Rhône River high in the Pennine Alps. Nuclear power plants provide a small percentage of Switzerland's energy needs, but this source has encountered resistance from environmental activists concerned about the safety of nuclear technology.

Switzerland imports the rest of its fuel. Crude petroleum comes from Libya and Great Britain, for example, and refined petroleum is imported from France and Germany. Dutch and German companies supply natural gas. To reduce air pollution, Switzerland has decreased its demand for imported petroleum through conservation and through the use of natural gas and nuclear energy.

Despite its rugged terrain, Switzerland has a well-developed system of roads and railways. The country's transportation network includes 43,500 miles of roads and

Photo by Mary Ney

Water spills from a Swiss hydroelectric power plant. By the late 1900s, Switzerland had developed virtually all the potential hydropower its rivers could produce.

Kein Plutonium für die Todesfabrik Sellafield
GREENPEACE

No Plutonium F Sellafield Death-
GREENPEACE

Photo by Reuters/Bettmann

Protesters from the environmental group Greenpeace put up crosses at a Swiss nuclear power plant to show their concerns about this type of energy.

Vehicles pass through the Great St. Bernard Tunnel, which connects Valais canton to Italy to the south. An extensive system of tunnels and bridges carries hundreds of thousands of automobiles through the Swiss Alps daily. The high volume of traffic on these roadways has caused many Swiss to worry about rising levels of air and noise pollution.

3,100 miles of railroads. This network connects even small, isolated villages with cities and towns.

Switzerland's system of highways and railways include hundreds of trans-Alpine tunnels, one of which stretches for more than 12 miles underneath the mountains at Simplon. To cut down on polluting truck traffic in the Alps, Swiss engineers are developing new railway tunnels that would allow freight containers to pass through the mountains by train.

The government-owned rail network in Switzerland links all major cities with high-speed trains. Five internationally connected railways also crisscross the nation, linking it with the rest of Europe. In the cities, the Swiss can take buses and trams to reach most locations. Small rail-ways and cable cars travel to high peaks in the Alps.

Because Switzerland is a landlocked country, export shipping does not play a major role in the economy. The Rhine River, with a port at Basel, carries nearly all the inland water shipments, most of which consist of bulk imports for Swiss industries. Large river barges reach Basel from the North Sea, transporting about eight million tons of cargo each year. On the nation's larger lakes, including Lake Geneva and Lake Lucerne, passenger ferries operate from April to October. Switzerland also has three airports that handle international flights—at Zurich, at Geneva, and at Bern—and one national carrier, Swissair. Three smaller airports offer domestic service.

Agriculture and Forestry

A small part of the Swiss economy, agriculture employs only 5 percent of the Swiss workforce. Even so, the government protects farmers by offering generous subsidies (payments) in the form of price guarantees, grants, and credits. Swiss farmers, in fact, receive 80 percent of their income from the government. The food grown in Switzerland makes up only 60 percent of the nation's requirements, however, so the rest must be purchased from foreign sources. Despite high tariffs on imported food, Switzerland buys more agricultural goods than any other European nation.

Farmlands occupy less than one-third of the Swiss landscape. Because mountains dominate the terrain, most farms are in the Mittelland, where small holdings stretch from Geneva to the German border. Cattle herding and small-scale farming take place in isolated valleys of the Alps. Overall, about 40 percent of the land devoted to agriculture is pasture, while the

Swiss cows graze on meadow grass in an Alpine valley. Cattle raising and dairying in Switzerland make up more than 70 percent of the country's agricultural output.

Photo by Janet Bennett

Fields of grain, potatoes, sugar beets, and vegetable crops stretch across the Mittelland.

Photo © Jeff Strong/Photo Agora

60

Terraced vineyards cover a steep hillside near Montreux in the French-speaking region of Switzerland.

rest supports mainly grain crops. Sales from the raising of livestock account for 75 percent of Switzerland's farm income.

Although Switzerland's production of milk, cheese, eggs, mutton, and beef mostly feeds local consumers, the country does export butter and several famous Swiss cheeses. Besides dairy livestock and cereal grains, Swiss farmers raise potatoes, sugar beets, apples, and grapes. Swiss vineyards produce a small variety of wines.

Forests cover about 25 percent of the nation's land, and logging employs about 4 percent of the workforce. The federal government owns most of the woodlands and

Stacks of logs and processed lumber lay idle in rural Switzerland, where many forests are dead or dying. Workers often cut down sick trees before they die to prevent the spreading of parasites that feed on the damaged trees.

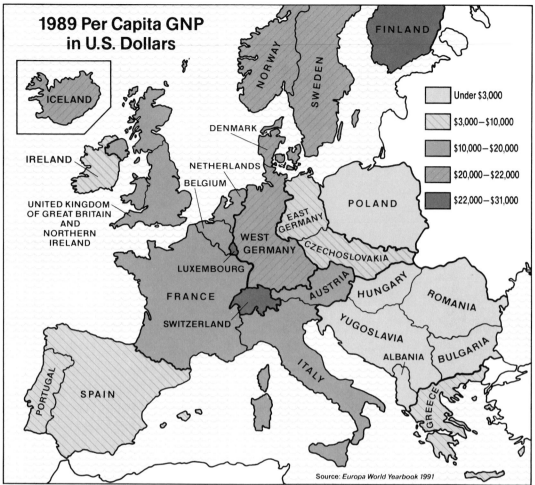

1989 Per Capita GNP in U.S. Dollars

Under $3,000

$3,000–$10,000

$10,000–$20,000

$20,000–$22,000

$22,000–$31,000

Source: *Europa World Yearbook 1991*

Artwork by Laura Westlund

This chart compares the average productivity per person—calculated by gross national product (GNP) per capita—for 26 European countries. The GNP is the value of all goods and services produced by a country in a year. To arrive at the GNP per capita, each nation's total GNP is divided by its population. The resulting dollar amounts indicate one measure of the standard of living in each country. In 1989 Switzerland's per capita GNP was about $31,000—the highest in Europe. Despite political changes on the continent, Switzerland has continued to be strong economically. Its 1995 per capita GNP of $36,410 is still the highest in Europe and one of the highest in the world.

considers forestry a small part of the Swiss economy. Harvesting of trees has been unusually high in the 1990s, because acid rain has damaged many forests. Crews are logging forests at a faster rate than ever before to ensure profits while the forests are still relatively healthy.

The Future

Modern Switzerland faces several future challenges. The federal government favors joining the European Union (EU), for example, but Swiss public opinion remains mixed. Those in favor of EU membership say that without it, the country will suffer economic hardship and isolation. Those who say the country should go it alone believe the EU would force Switzerland to abandon its time-honored traditions of direct democracy and neutrality.

In the mid-1990s, the nation's economy slowed, unemployment rose, the social-security system lost money, and crime increased. For some Swiss, these factors suggest that the country's social fabric is starting to fray. Yet Switzerland's problems are not as bad as those of many other European countries. The Swiss unemployment rate remains low at around 5 percent, and money from tourism continues to pour in. With a well-educated workforce, a strong and diverse economy, and a stable democratic government, Switzerland appears well equipped to handle the challenges of the twenty-first century.

A group of young people look out over the Limnat River and the heart of Zurich.

Index